Summer Bridge Reading
Grades 1-2

Y0-BDB-748

Editors: Heather Canup, Julie Kirsch
Layout Design: Tiara Reynolds
Inside Illustrations: Andy Carlson
Cover Design: Chasity Rice
Cover Illustration: Wayne Miller

ISBN 978-1-60022-444-7

Table of Contents

The *Summer Bridge Reading* series is designed to help children improve their reading skills during the summer months and between grades. *Summer Bridge Reading* includes several extra components to help make your child's study of reading easier and more inviting.

For example, an **Assessment** test has been included to help you determine your child's reading knowledge and what skills need improvement. Use this test, as well as the **Assessment Analysis**, as a diagnostic tool for those areas in which your child may need extra practice.

Furthermore, the **Incentive Contract** will motivate your child to complete the work in *Summer Bridge Reading*. Together, you and your child choose the reward for completing specific sections of the book. Check off the pages that your child has completed, and he or she will have a record of accomplishment.

Examples are included for each new skill that your child will learn. The examples are located in blue boxes at the tops of the pages. On each page, the directions refer to the example your child needs to complete a specific type of activity.

Same and Different

Circle the word that means the same as the bold word. This is called a synonym. **Synonyms** are words that have the same meaning.

1. My mother bought me a **pretty** dress.

   old   (beautiful)   ugly

2. I can not find my red baseball **cap**.

   (hat)   top   jacket

3. Since I'm not feeling well, I will **rest**.

   eat   play   (sleep)

4. My little brother loves to **jump** in mud puddles.

   (hop)   walk   run

5. My best friend always **giggles** at my jokes.

   (laughs)   grumbles   cries

Draw a line from each word on the right to the word on the left with the opposite meaning. This is called an antonym. **Antonyms** are words that have opposite meanings.

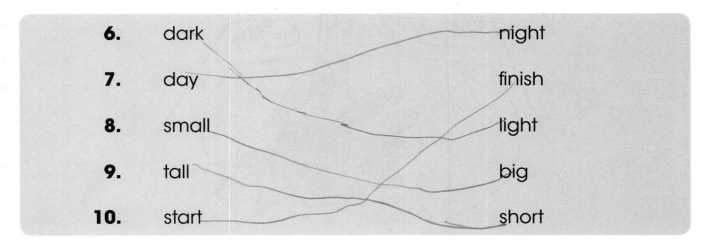

6. dark   night

7. day   finish

8. small   light

9. tall   big

10. start   short

9

Read the passage below.

Germs are things you should not share. Germs can make you sick. Even though you cannot see germs, they get into the body in many ways. Germs get in the body through the nose, mouth, eyes, and cuts in the skin. We share germs when we sneeze or cough and do not cover our mouths. We share germs when we drink from the same cup or eat from the same plate.

To keep germs to yourself and to get well:
- Wash your hands with soap.
- Cover your mouth when you cough or sneeze.
- Do not share food or drink.
- Keep your fingers away from your nose, mouth, and eyes.
- Drink lots of water.
- Get lots of fresh air.
- Eat healthy meals.
- Get plenty of sleep.

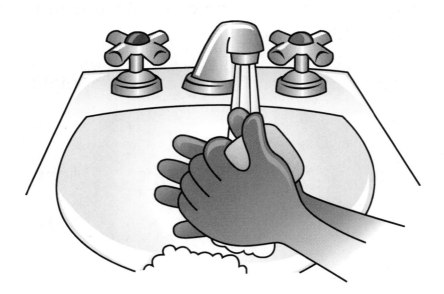

Answer the following questions using the passage on page 10.

1. What is the main idea?

A. (Germs are things you do not want to share.)

B. You can't see germs.

C. Wash your hands often.

2. Put an *X* next to the ways you can keep germs to yourself.

___X___ Wash your hands with soap.

___X___ Stay away from animals.

___X___ Cover your mouth when you cough or sneeze.

___F___ Get plenty of sleep.

___F___ Eat healthy meals.

3. Put a *T* next to the sentences that are true. Put an *F* next to the sentences that are false.

___T___ Germs can make you sick.

___F___ Germs cannot get in your body through the nose, mouth, eyes, and cuts in the skin.

___T___ Cover your mouth when you cough or sneeze to keep germs to yourself.

Choose the correct short vowel.

4. Germs can make you s _i_ ck.

i   o

5. Germs get in the body through c _u_ ts in the skin.

a   u

6. Cover your mo _u_ th when you cough.

o   u

7. Get l _o_ ts of fresh air.

i   o

Use the dictionary entry below to answer the questions.

> **germ** (jûrm), n. 1. a disease-producing microbe. 2. a bud or seed.

8. What part of speech is *germ*?

_____morthing_____

9. Use the word *germ* in a sentence.

_____elly wynt to_____

_____The park_____

_____A might Found a pet germ._____

Abby

Read the story below.

My dog, Abby, loves to go to the river. Every Saturday morning, I take Abby to the park by the river to play. The first thing Abby does when we get there is run down to the water.

Abby likes to splash in the water. The cold water doesn't bother her. When she gets out of the water, she shakes and shakes. I stand back so that the water does not get on me. Then, she looks for a rock in the sun to take a nap on. She sleeps there until I whistle for her when it is time to go home.

I think our Saturday trips to the river are something that Abby looks forward to all week.

Answer the following questions using the story on page 12.

1. What is the main idea?
   A. Abby takes a nap.
   B. Abby loves trips to the river.
   C. Abby is a good dog.

2. Number the events in the order that they happened in the story.
   ___ I whistle for Abby when it is time to go home.
   ___ Abby runs to the water.
   ___ Abby takes a nap.
   ___ Abby splashes in the water.

3. What does Abby do when she gets out of the water?
   A. rolls in the dirt
   B. shakes and shakes
   C. licks her fur

Choose the correct short vowel.

4. I have a d ___ g.
   i   o

5. Abby likes to spl ___ sh in the water.
   a   i

6. Abby n ___ ps on a rock.
   i   a

7. Abby finds a rock in the s ___ n.
   u   a

Sometimes the same word can be used as a noun or as a verb. Write *noun* or *verb* to tell how the bold word is used in each sentence.

8. Can I have a **drink**, please?

_____

9. My dogs **drink** a lot of water.

_____

10. My dog made a big **splash** in the water.

_____

11. The children **splash** in the water.

_____

12. I order a **shake** with my burger.

_____

13. My hands **shake** when I am nervous.

_____

Watch That Vowel!

In some words with two vowels that are together, the first vowel makes a long sound, and the second vowel is silent.

Look at these double vowel words:

road   faint

rōad   fāint

Watch for the vowel *i* followed by the silent *g*:

night

nīght

Circle the word that describes each picture.

1. hēar / hāy	**2.** pāint / pănt	**3.** weēd / wĕd
4. bĕt / bēet	**5.** līght / lĭt	**6.** bēan / bĕn
7. pāid / păd	**8.** rough / rīght	**9.** cŏt / cōat
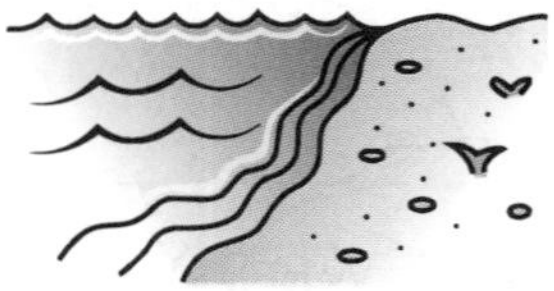 **10.** cōast / cŏst	**11.** 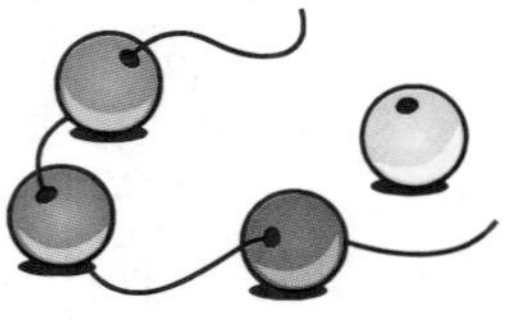 beads / beds	**12.** mĕt / mēat
13. gōat / gŏt	**14.** rĕd / rēad	**15.** trāy / trāin

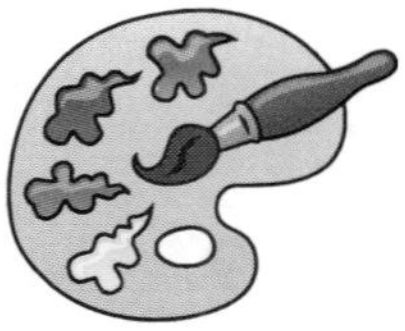

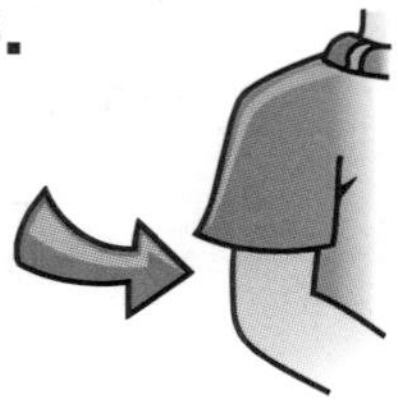

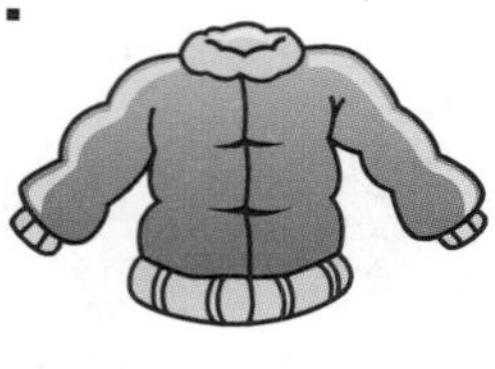

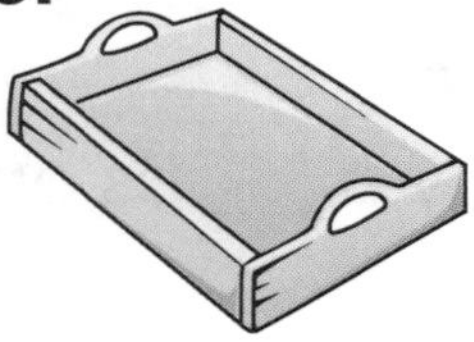

Summer Bridge Reading RB-904092

Read the poem below.

Mom and Dad think I'm too old
to still have my teddy bear.
They say, "You are eight years old now,
and Teddy shows too much wear."
I nod my head and then agree.
I know I'm a real strong kid.
Without a thought I put him up,
and in my closet he hid.

That same night, I tried and tried,
but could not fall asleep.
A storm came in with lots of noise.
I did not make a peep.
Instead, I took my bear out
of the hiding place I made.
I did not need him to fall asleep.
I just knew he was afraid.

Answer the following questions using the poem on page 15. Circle your choice.

1. Why do the parents want the child to put the teddy bear away?

    A. They think that the child is too old to have a teddy bear.

    B. They think that the child will lose the bear.

    C. They want the child to play with other toys.

    D. They think that teddy bears are silly.

2. Why couldn't the child in the poem fall asleep?

    A. The child was cold.

    B. The child was worried that the parents were angry.

    C. The child was hungry.

    D. The child thought that the teddy bear was afraid.

3. What did the child do when there was a storm?

    A. went into Mom and Dad's room

    B. got the teddy bear

    C. cried

    D. hid under the covers

4. *Kid* and *hid* are words that rhyme in the poem. Which two words in the pairs below do not rhyme?

    A. *fun* and *run*   **B.** *bike* and *ride*

    C. *bear* and *tear*   **D.** *hide* and *side*

5. *Asleep* and *peep* are words in the poem that make the long *e* sound. Which word below does not have the long *e* sound?

    A. read   **B.** see

    C. agree   **D.** bed

16

Twins

Read the story below.

Greg and Tim are twins. They are brothers who were born on the same day. Twins that look almost exactly alike are called identical twins. Greg and Tim do look alike, but they are not identical twins. Greg and Tim are fraternal twins. That means they were born on the same day but do not look exactly alike.

Tim has curly red hair. Greg's hair is brown and straight. Greg has green eyes. Tim's eyes are blue. Another difference between them is their teeth. Greg is missing his two front teeth. Tim has all of his teeth, and he has braces!

Both boys like to play baseball. Sometimes, they play third base. Sometimes, they play catcher. Both of them can throw the ball well. It can be fun to have a twin.

Summer Bridge Reading RB-904092

Twins

Answer the following questions using the story on page 17. Read each phrase. If it describes Greg, write a *G* on the line. If it describes Tim, write a *T* on the line. If the phrase describes both boys, write a *B* on the line.

1. is a twin _____

2. has red hair _____

3. plays catcher _____

4. missing two front teeth _____

5. has green eyes _____

6. Draw a picture of each boy.

7. What do you call twins that do not look exactly alike?

_____

8. Circle the words below that have a long vowel sound.

twin	red	base
teeth	play	fun
braces	Tim	both

Pandas at the Zoo

The **main idea** of a story tells what the story is about. It does not tell one part of the story or recall one fact from the story. It is an overview of the entire story or paragraph. Titles often tell you something about the main idea.

The titles below describe the main ideas for the stories on page 20. Look closely at the titles. Write each title at the top of its matching story. Remember to ask yourself, "Does this title tell about the whole story?"

When Yang Yang Is Sick	The Panda Keeper
Becoming a Zookeeper	What Yang Yang Eats

Summer Bridge Reading RB-904092

Pandas at the Zoo

See directions on page 19.

1.	**2.**
Brenda Morgan is a zookeeper in Washington, D.C. Brenda has the very important job of caring for a panda named Yang Yang at the zoo. She is in charge of making sure Yang Yang is happy and healthy.	Brenda always wanted to work closely with animals and help care for them. As a child, Brenda wanted to be a horse when she grew up! Since she could not become a horse, she became a zookeeper instead. Brenda loves her job at the zoo.
3.	**4.**
Part of Brenda's job is to watch Yang Yang closely to be sure he is feeling well. Once, he had an eye infection, and Yang Yang went blind for a few days. Brenda called the veterinarian for medicine, and now Yang Yang is well again.	Yang Yang eats many kinds of foods. He likes gruel, which is made of rice, honey, and cheese. He also enjoys apples and bamboo. Brenda thinks his favorite food is carrots.

Insects

Read each paragraph. Read the sentences. Then, circle the main idea of each paragraph.

1. All insects have six legs. Butterflies and bees have six legs. They are insects. Spiders have eight legs. They are not insects.

   A. Spiders are not insects.

   B. Bees are insects.

   C. Insects have six legs.

2. Insects eat different things. Some insects eat plants. Caterpillars eat leaves. Bees and butterflies eat the nectar of flowers. Some insects eat other insects. Ladybugs eat aphids. Ant lions eat ants.

   A. Ladybugs eat aphids.

   B. Insects eat different things.

   C. Butterflies eat nectar.

3. Insects live in different kinds of homes. Bees build hives out of wax. Ants and termites build hills on the ground. Some insects, like mayflies and damselflies, live underwater. Other insects live under rocks or in old logs.

   A. Insects live in different kinds of homes.

   B. Some insects live underwater.

   C. Some insects build hills.

Summer Bridge Reading RB-904092

Noah's Tadpoles

Read each paragraph. Then, circle the main idea.

1. It was spring. The breeze was soft and warm. The grass on the hills was green. White clouds floated across the blue sky.

    A. The grass was green.

    B. The sky was blue.

    C. It was spring.

2. Noah went outside to play. His ball rolled near the fish pond. Noah had not looked at the pond since fall. He stopped to see the fish. There were four goldfish. There were also some new fish. They were small and dark. Noah ran back to his house to get his dad.

    A. Noah liked to play ball.

    B. Noah saw new fish in the pond.

    C. Noah had four goldfish.

3. Noah's dad came out to look at the new fish. He said they were not fish at all. He said they were tadpoles. He told Noah that the tadpoles would grow bigger and bigger. He said that in a month or two, they would grow legs. The tadpoles would grow up to be frogs.

    A. The new fish were tadpoles.

    B. The tadpoles would grow legs.

    C. Noah's dad put new fish in the pond.

Chemicals

Longer stories can be written in paragraphs. Each paragraph tells about something different. The title of the story should be about the entire story. Each paragraph will have a main idea that describes that paragraph.

Chemicals are everywhere. They make up our air, our houses, our food, and even our bodies. Chemicals help make everything different. They make apples sweet and lemons sour. They make leaves green in spring and red, orange, and yellow in fall.

When chemicals mix to form something new, it is called a *reaction*. As a banana ripens, it changes from green to yellow. This is from chemicals changing. When you mix chocolate with milk, you are watching chemicals change in a tasty way!

Circle a title to describe the passage above. Then, circle a main idea to describe each paragraph.

1. A good title for this story would be:
   A. Chemicals in Our Bodies
   B. Why Bananas Change Color
   C. Chemicals Around Us

2. The first paragraph is mostly about:
   A. Apples are sweet.
   B. Chemicals are everywhere.
   C. Leaves are green.

3. The second paragraph is mostly about:
   A. Chemicals can cause changes.
   B. Bananas turn from green to yellow.
   C. Chocolate milk is tasty.

Crystal's Backpack

Some details are written as descriptive words (adjectives and adverbs). When you read for details, pay close attention to the descriptive words.

Crystal waved good-bye to her parents and threw her striped backpack over her shoulder. She found her best friend, Sarah, on the bus and sat next to her. "Camp will be so much fun," Sarah said, "but I think I will miss my family."

Crystal unzipped her backpack. "Maybe an apple will help you feel better," she said.

The girls finished their snack in no time. They watched out the window as busy highways became small roads and buildings became lakes. "This makes me feel homesick," Sarah said as she slumped down.

"I have cards in the pocket of my backpack. Should we play?" Crystal asked.

"Okay," answered Sarah. She beat Crystal twice. By the time they started their third game, Sarah had forgotten all about being homesick.

Use details from the story to find which backpack below belongs to Crystal. Circle it. You may want to reread the story, watching for details about the backpack.

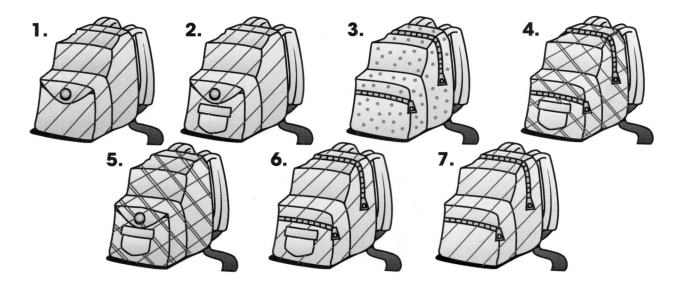

Pretty Pancakes!

Recognizing details means being able to find specific answers to questions about a story.

Butterflies are lovely to look at, but here is how to make one you can eat!

You will need:

    2 frozen pancakes
    1 banana
    2 grapes
    2 sausage links
    jelly or jam
    2 toothpicks

Directions:

- Toast two pancakes and cut them in half. Arrange the pieces on a plate to look like the four wings of a butterfly.

- Peel the banana and place it on the plate. This will be the butterfly's body.

- Spread jelly or jam on the "wings."

- Use the toothpicks to hold the grapes like eyes on the banana.

- Cook the sausage. Then, place it at the top of the banana as antennae.

Use details from the story to fill in the missing words.

1. The _____ will make the butterfly's body.

2. The wings will be covered with _____.

3. Butterflies have four _____.

4. The antennae will be made from _____.

5. A butterfly has two _____ to see with.

Josh and the Bear

Read the story. Circle *True* if a sentence is true. Circle *False* if it is false.

Josh heard something outside in the woods. It was still dark. Ma and Pa were sleeping. Josh lit the candle by his bed. There was no window in the little cabin. Josh went to the front door and looked out. Little dark eyes looked back at him. The little dark eyes were part of a big, dark face.

Slam! Josh shut the door. He put the big wooden bar across it.

He ran over to the bed and shook his father. "Pa," he said. "Hurry! Bear!" He was too scared to say anything else.

Ma and Pa sat up in bed. Suddenly, they heard a polite knock on the door. Then, the bear began to sing. Josh peeked through the keyhole. He saw the bear juggling four apples.

1.	Josh was afraid.	True	False
2.	The thing at the door was a mountain lion.	True	False
3.	Josh closed the door and put a wooden bar across it.	True	False
4.	Josh was awake before Pa.	True	False
5.	This story could have taken place a long time ago.	True	False
6.	The story takes place at noon.	True	False
7.	The story is real.	True	False

Extra!

What happened next? _____

_____

_____

A Great Castle!

Read the story below.

Jessica and Alex are building a castle. Jessica builds the walls with brown wooden squares. Alex adds the green triangle roof. Jessica balances the long yellow cylinder towers. Alex tops them with red cones. Jessica puts blue rectangles inside for beds. Alex builds a path with small orange cubes. At last they are finished. That is great teamwork!

Mark an X in each box to show which child used each shape.

Shapes	Jessica	Alex
triangles		
rectangles		
squares		
cylinders		
cubes		
cones		

Draw the castle.

Summer Bridge Reading RB-904092

What Does It Mean?

Sometimes, **context clues** will help you make a good guess at a word's meaning. Context clues are other words that show you the unknown word's meaning.

Use the context clues to make the best choice for each bold word's meaning. Circle your choice.

1. The blue paint turned a **pale** color when I added water to it.

    bright   light   green

2. My brother found a **blade** of grass on his shoe.

    piece   handle   wheel

3. Dad likes to relax on the **sofa** after he takes us swimming.

    bike   couch   stairs

4. Would you like a large or a small **slice** of watermelon?

    plate   piece   picnic

5. Prairie dogs sit on **mounds** to help them see danger coming.

    their tails   small hills   chairs

6. The aquarium has many **rare** fish that would be hard to see anywhere else.

    special   large   scary

7. The cowboy tried to **calm** the horses after the loud thunder ended.

    quiet   move   saddle

Summer Bridge Reading RB-904092

Figuring It Out!

Use context clues in each sentence to help you choose the meaning of the bold word. Circle your choice.

1. It was a **pleasant** day. The sky was blue and the sun was warm. We put on our swimsuits. We ran down to the beach.

   dull   nice   sad

2. It was hot outside. Toby went to gather some eggs. All of the hens were asleep **beneath** the porch.

   under   above   with

3. Irma fell down in the yard during lunch. She hurt her arm. The **ache** got worse when she carried a big box for Mrs. Wilson.

   dream   page   pain

4. Some dinosaurs were small, but brachiosaurs were **huge**.

   fast   big   old

5. We would not let a little rain **spoil** our trip to the zoo. We took our raincoats and umbrellas.

   ruin   fix   share

6. It was Clara's birthday. She was happy. She knew she would **receive** a gift from her best friend.

   give   chose   get

Extra!

On another piece of paper, write a paragraph that uses the word *assisting*. The paragraph should have context clues that show what the word means.

29

Makes Sense

Read each pair of sentences. Find a word in the first sentence that makes sense in the second sentence. Write the word on the line.

1. Jabar planted carrots in his garden.

His sister loved to eat _____.

2. It was a relief to finish the test.

It was a _____ to get a good grade.

3. They were the toughest team in town.

They had the _____ first baseman.

4. A thief stole some of the lunch money.

Nobody trusts a _____ with money.

5. Danny had to go home because of an emergency.

A fire is an _____.

Extra!

On another piece of paper, write a paragraph about an emergency. The paragraph should have context clues that show what the word means.

Balloon Words

Complete the sentences. Use the words in the balloons below.

1. My uncle's job is to be a circus _____ .

2. He paints a big, red _____ on his face.

3. He makes animals by blowing up and tying _____ .

4. He goes to parties and makes children _____ .

5. At _____ , I like to look at the stars.

6. The _____ make pictures in the sky called constellations.

7. Some groups of stars look like _____ .

8. I always wish on the _____ star I see.

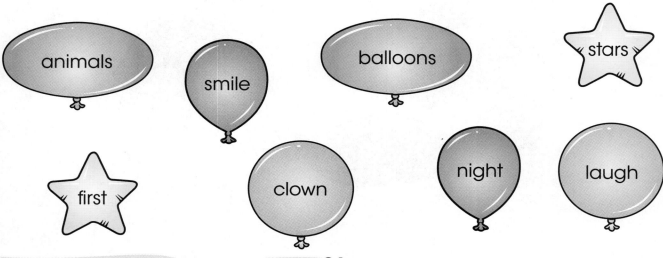

Summer Bridge Reading RB-904092

The Ladybug

Read the passages below.

The ladybug is also called a ladybird beetle. It is a very interesting insect. Most ladybugs are red or yellow with black spots. The California ladybug's shell is yellow with black spots. The ladybug has a tiny head and no neck. Its body is round and shaped like half of a pea. It can run very fast on its short legs. The ladybug's wings are tucked under its shell. It can fly very well.

The ladybug lays its eggs on the underside of green leaves. When the grubs hatch, they are very hungry. They quickly start to eat plant lice. Lice are insects that can ruin a farmer's crop. Fruit growers like ladybugs because they eat harmful lice.

The California ladybug was brought to the United States from Australia. It helps protect orange, lemon, and grapefruit trees.

The Ladybug

Answer the following questions using the passage on page 32.

1. What is true about ladybugs?
    A. They have big heads.
    B. They have long necks.
    C. They can fly.

2. Where does the ladybug lay its eggs?
    A. in a nest
    B. on the underside of a leaf
    C. on the bark of a tree

3. What type of animal is a ladybug?
    A. an insect
    B. a bird
    C. can not tell from the story

4. What do grubs eat?
    A. leaves
    B. fruit
    C. lice

5. In this story, a grub is _____.
    A. something to eat
    B. a baby ladybug
    C. a leaf

6. **Proper nouns** are specific names of persons, places, or things. Proper nouns always begin with uppercase letters. Find three proper nouns in the last paragraph.

    _____

    _____

    _____

7. Words in an index are listed alphabetically. Number these words as they would appear in the index of a book about ladybugs.

    ___ larva

    ___ beetles

    ___ lice

    ___ grub

    ___ insects

    ___ eggs

    ___ wings

33

A Real King

> **Characters** are the people, animals, or animated objects in a story. They are brought to life by their actions, and they may even change in the story as people do in real life.

Larry the Lion had been king of the grasslands for a very long time. But the animals felt that they needed a new king. King Larry had become lazy, mean, and selfish. When King Larry learned of how the animals felt, he set them free and laughed to himself, "They will beg to have me back!" The animals did not beg to have Larry back, and so he moved away.

One lonely day, Larry found a mouse that was balancing on a branch over the river. He helped the mouse to the shore. Later, Larry found a baby zebra who was lost. Larry was kind and helped the little zebra find his home.

When the animals learned of Larry's kind acts, they asked him to become their king again. They needed a helpful and strong king, which Larry now seemed to be. King Larry had become a real king!

Did you notice that King Larry's character changed as the story continued? Complete the lists below by writing three words to describe King Larry at the beginning of the story. Then, write three words to describe King Larry at the end of the story.

King Larry at the Beginning

1. _____
2. _____
3. _____

King Larry at the End

4. _____
5. _____
6. _____

34

City Mouse, Country Mouse

Stories with more than one important character can be more fun to read. The main characters are usually different from each other, just as the people you know are different.

Once upon a time, a city mouse went to visit her friend in the country. The country mouse spent the day gathering grain and dried pieces of corn in order to greet her friend with a nice meal. The city mouse was surprised to find her friend living in a cold tree stump and eating scraps. So, she invited the country mouse to visit her in the city. The country mouse agreed.

The country mouse could not believe her eyes when she arrived! Her friend lived in a warm hole behind the fireplace of a large home. She was even more surprised to find all of the fine foods that were left behind after a party the night before. The country mouse wished that she could live in the city as well.

Suddenly, the family's cat ran in and chased the two mice. He nearly caught the country mouse with his sharp claws. As the friends raced back to the mouse hole, the country mouse said, "I'm sorry, friend, but I would rather live a simple life eating corn and grain than live a fancy life in fear!" The country mouse went back home.

The two characters in this story are different from each other. Mark an *X* in each box to describe the correct mouse.

		City Mouse	Country Mouse
1.	She feasted on fine foods.		
2.	She would rather have a simple, safe life.		
3.	She gathered grain and corn.		
4.	She lived in a large house.		
5.	She was surprised by all of the fine foods.		
6.	She lived in a warm place.		

35

Feelings

To make stories more interesting, characters often face issues that can be good or bad. A character shows feelings by what he says or does.

Each of the children below feels a certain way. Read each sign for clues. Use the words from the word bank to complete the signs. You will not use all of the words.

| scared | proud | worried | disappointed | excited |

1. I watched a movie about ghosts last night. Now, I feel _____ .

2. I forgot my backpack on the bus. I'm _____ about getting it back.

3. I worked hard and spelled every word the correct way on my test. I feel _____ .

4. I'm so _____ it rained on the day of my big game.

The Lonely Turtle

Read the story below.

Thomas was a turtle who lived with his mother near a creek. The creek was full of other living creatures. But no one was Thomas's age. Day in and day out, Thomas tried to fit in with the older critters. He tried racing with the raccoons. They were much faster than Thomas. He tried climbing trees with the possums, but turtles aren't made to climb. Thomas nearly broke his shell when he fell from one of the lower branches!

To fill his time, Thomas started painting rocks. He painted little rocks and big rocks. He painted flat rocks and round rocks. Sometimes, he painted a design. Other times, he painted pictures of the other animals that lived near the creek. Thomas was so worried about finding someone just like him to play with that he didn't notice how beautiful his paintings were. Instead of keeping the rocks, he simply tossed them into the creek.

Weeks went by, and all that Thomas did was paint. His mother started to worry about him. The more she tried to talk to Thomas, the more he ran off to paint. Talking about his feelings upset Thomas, and he did not want his mother to see him cry.

One afternoon, Thomas tossed his latest painted rock into the creek. He was startled when a large frog hopped out of the water and onto the bank. "Watch out!" the frog yelled. "I'm sorry," said Thomas. "I didn't see you there."

The Lonely Turtle

"That's OK," said the frog. "I shouldn't have surprised you like that. I just wanted to catch your next rock." "Why would you want to do a thing like that?" asked Thomas. "You don't know?" asked the frog. "Your work is beautiful! Every frog in the creek looks for your rocks. They are treasures."

"Really?" asked Thomas. "Sure! Come with me," the frog said.

Thomas and the frog swam down the creek together. Thomas was amazed when he saw the frog's house. It was covered in Thomas's rocks! It was beautiful! The frog introduced Thomas to his friends. They had Thomas's painted rocks on their houses, too. Everyone was happy to meet the artist they admired so much. One frog even asked Thomas for his autograph!

When Thomas got home, he told his mother the whole story. She was thrilled to see her little boy happy again. Thomas and his new friends spent afternoons playing in the creek and painting rocks. He was no longer a lonely turtle.

38

The Lonely Turtle

After reading "The Lonely Turtle," answer the following questions. Circle your choice.

1. What was Thomas's problem?
    A. The raccoons were faster than he was.
    B. He didn't have any friends.
    C. He couldn't paint well.
    D. The possums made fun of him.

2. What did Thomas do to pass the time?
    A. He talked to his mom.
    B. He drew pictures.
    C. He climbed trees with the possums.
    D. He painted rocks.

3. Why was the frog waiting in the creek?
    A. He wanted to catch one of Thomas's rocks.
    B. He was afraid of Thomas.
    C. He was hiding from his friends.
    D. He wanted to learn how to paint.

4. How do you think Thomas felt when he saw the frog's house? Why?

    _____

5. Do you think that Thomas continued to paint rocks after he met the frog? Why or why not?

    _____

Super Sport

> **Sequencing** means putting events from a story in the order that they happened.

Read "Super Sport." Then, read the sentences below. Write a number in front of each sentence to show the order in which they happened.

In December 1891, at McGill University in Springfield, MA, Dr. James Naismith nailed a peach basket onto a 10-foot pole. In order to keep his students occupied and healthy during the long New England winters, he created a new indoor game that would later be named basketball.

In 1892, Senda Berenson, a physical education teacher at Smith College, modified Naismith's rules so that her female students could play the new game.

The first official basketball game was played in a YMCA gymnasium on January 20, 1892. The game had nine players and was on a court half the size of today's standard court.

The National Basketball Association (NBA) was formed in 1946 with 11 teams. The first game was played on November 1, 1946 between the Toronto Huskies and the New York Knickerbockers. The Women's National Basketball Association (WNBA) began in 1997 with eight teams. The first season began on June 21, 1997.

_____ The National Basketball Association was formed.

_____ Dr. James Naismith created a new game for his students.

_____ The first official basketball game was played.

_____ The Women's National Basketball association began.

_____ Senda Berenson modified the game for her female students.

_____ The Toronto Huskies played the New York Knickerbockers.

The Gingerbread Boy

Read the story below.

One day, a woman decided to bake gingerbread into the shape of a boy. She placed raisins for eyes and licorice for the mouth. She used cinnamon candies for the buttons on his vest. When she was satisfied, she popped her little gingerbread boy into the oven. Soon, she could smell the delicious scent of warm gingerbread. She opened the oven door, and the little gingerbread boy popped out.

"Yum! You smell delicious," sighed the old woman.

"Run, run, as fast as you can. You can't catch me. I'm too fast, you see!" the gingerbread boy laughed, and he ran away.

"Oh my!" screamed the little old woman, and she ran after her little gingerbread boy.

The little gingerbread boy came to a young boy. "Yum! You smell delicious!" shouted the boy.

But, the gingerbread boy just laughed and said, "Run, run, as fast as you can. You can't catch me. I'm too fast, you see!" And the little gingerbread boy ran away with the little old woman and the boy close behind.

The little gingerbread boy came to a girl. "Yum! You smell delicious!" squealed the girl.

But the gingerbread boy just laughed and said, "Run, run, as fast as you can. You can't catch me. I'm too fast, you see!" The gingerbread boy ran away with the old woman, the boy, and the girl close behind.

Soon, the gingerbread boy came to a man. "Yum! You smell delicious!" bellowed the man.

But the gingerbread boy just laughed and said, "Run, run, as fast as you can. You can't catch me. I'm too fast, you see!" And the gingerbread boy ran away with the old woman, the boy, the girl, and the man close behind.

Soon, the gingerbread boy came to a river. "Oh dear," said the gingerbread boy. "How will I cross this river?"

"I'll give you a ride," snickered an alligator with a sly smile. "Just jump on my back."

The gingerbread boy accepted the alligator's offer. As you might expect, the gingerbread boy didn't make it across the river, but instead made it into the belly of the alligator.

When the old woman, the boy, the girl, and the man reached the river, they knew immediately what had happened. "Let's go home," sighed the old woman. "I will make some gingerbread for us. Just a plain loaf of gingerbread."

The Gingerbread Boy

After reading "The Gingerbread Boy," answer the following questions.

1. Number the sentences to show the order in which they happened in the story.

    ___ The old woman baked a plain loaf of gingerbread.

    ___ The old woman chased the gingerbread boy.

    ___ The old woman cut her gingerbread into the shape of a boy.

    ___ The boy chased the gingerbread boy.

    ___ The alligator ate the gingerbread boy.

    ___ The girl chased the gingerbread boy.

    ___ The man chased the gingerbread boy.

    ___ The gingerbread boy came to a river.

2. Find six words that were used in place of the word *said* in the story.

    _____   _____

    _____   _____

    _____   _____

Read the recipe card below. Then, answer the questions.

Gingerbread Cookies

1 cup molasses	1 tsp. baking soda
½ cup brown sugar	2 tsp. ginger
⅓ cup water	1 tsp. cinnamon
⅓ cup shortening	1 tsp. all spice
6 cups flour	

1. Mix together the molasses, brown sugar, water, and shortening.
2. Sift together flour, soda, and spices. Then, add to molasses mixture. Cover and refrigerate overnight.
3. Heat oven to 350°F. Roll out dough on a floured board. Use cookie cutters to cut shapes. Place cookies on a cookie sheet. Bake 10–12 minutes.

Makes 2 dozen cookies.

3. How many cups of flour will you need? _____

4. How hot should the oven be?

    _____

5. How long do you need to bake the cookies?

    _____

6. How many cookies will this recipe make?

    _____

What Does It Tell You?

Many stories have a **cause and effect** that help you understand why things happen in the stories. Think about the story "Little Red Riding Hood."

Cause (what made it happen): It was really the wolf dressed up as Little Red Riding Hood's grandma!

Effect (what happened): Little Red Riding Hood thought that her grandma looked strange.

Read the cause below. Then, find the effect for each cause. Write each matching letter in the correct blank.

Cause	Effect
_____ **1.** The snowstorm lasted for two days.	**A.** Two pigs ran to their brother's house.
_____ **2.** Jack planted the magic beans.	**B.** Schools were closed last Thursday and Friday.
_____ **3.** Someone broke his little chair.	**C.** Tara's dog jumped out of the tub.
_____ **4.** The wolf blew their houses down.	**D.** The little bear was upset.
_____ **5.** She did not like taking a bath.	**E.** A huge bean stalk grew toward the sky.

6. Write your own cause and effect sentences below.

_____

_____

_____

Summer Bridge Reading RB-904092

What's the Cause?

Read each pair of sentences. Write *C* on the line if a sentence tells about the cause. Write *E* on the line if it tells about the effect.

1. The wind blew hard. _____
Dust was in the air. _____

2. The balloon popped. _____
Rosa blew more and more air into the balloon. _____

3. The clown kept making faces. _____
Everyone laughed. _____

4. We found the perfect book. _____
We went to the library. _____

5. I turned on the lamp. _____
It was light in the room. _____

Extra!

Read the effect. Then, write the cause. Use the words below to help you.

Effect: Daniel had to sit on the bench at recess.

Cause: _____

_____

| talking | late | passing | finish |
| homework | forgot | friend | notes |

Why Did This Happen?

Read each pair of sentences. Circle the sentence that tells the cause.

1. I came early.

I was first in line.

2. It broke.

The glass fell on the floor.

3. I went to see the nurse.

I felt sick.

4. We could not have a campfire.

The grass was very wet.

5. I got wet.

I fell in the river.

6. He hopped away.

The rabbit saw us.

7. The weeds grew fast.

We had to pull them up.

Extra!

Read the cause. Then, write the effect. Use the words below to help you.

Cause: **The camper did not pour water on his campfire.**

Effect: _____

_____

spread	burned	blew	grass
trees	firefighters	trucks	wind

Summer Bridge Reading RB-904092

April's Song

Read the story below.

April was excited to try out for the play. For weeks and weeks she practiced all of her lines in front of a mirror. The play had two main parts: a deer and a butterfly. April wanted the part of the butterfly.

Tryouts were on Friday. Thursday night, April had a hard time getting to sleep. "What if I forget my lines?" she asked herself. Finally, Friday arrived. After lunch, all of the students who wanted to try out for the play were asked to go to the auditorium. Sally went first. She wanted to be the deer. She did a great job. April hoped that she would do as well as Sally. Next, it was Albert's turn. He was trying out for the part of the butterfly. Albert did a great job, too. Then, it was April's turn. She walked onto the stage. Mrs. Johnson, the music teacher, asked her to say her lines. April was speechless. She could not say a word. Her mouth was dry, and she felt sick. April had stage fright!

When April got home, she cried as she told her parents what happened. Her mother said that when she was a little girl, she was afraid to talk in front of people, too. April was relieved that she was not the only person with stage fright.

The next day, Mrs. Johnson gave out parts in the play. Sally got the part of the deer. Albert got the part of the butterfly. April's part was a violet. After all of her practicing, April would be a flower in the school play. She was very disappointed.

April's main job was to hold a welcome sign at the edge of the stage. She did not have any lines. Even though her grandmother made her a beautiful violet costume, April was not excited when it was time for the play. "Why do I have to go?" she asked her parents. "All of the other kids have lines. The audience will laugh at me." April's parents reminded her that all of the parts in the play were important.

April's Song

On the night of the play, April went to her place on stage early. She decided that she would be the best violet the school had ever seen. She smiled throughout the play. At the end of the play, Allison, the narrator, was supposed to come onto the stage and thank everyone for coming. However, Allison was nowhere to be found!

Out of the corner of her eye, April noticed Mrs. Johnson waving at her. She was trying to tell her something. April realized that Mrs. Johnson was trying to tell her to thank the audience. Before she realized what she was doing, April began singing out loud. She was singing, "Good night, thank you for coming. Good night, we hope you enjoyed the show. Good night, we thank you all for coming. Good night, it's time for you to go!"

Everyone clapped and cheered. They loved April's song! It was a wonderful way to end the play. Mrs. Johnson thought that April did such a great job, she asked her to sing the same ending for the other shows.

April realized that when she sang on stage, she was not as frightened as when she tried to talk. She ended each show with her song, and even added a dance for the last performance. Being a flower was not a bad thing after all.

Summer Bridge Reading RB-904092

April's Song

After reading "April's Song," answer the following questions. Circle your choice.

1. What part did April want in the play?
    A. the violet
    B. the deer
    C. the butterfly
    D. the narrator

2. Why didn't April get the part she wanted?
    A. She yelled her lines.
    B. She had stage fright.
    C. She did not practice for her part.
    D. She sang her lines instead of speaking.

3. Why wasn't April excited on the night of the play?
    A. She did not like her costume.
    B. She did not know her lines.
    C. She was mad at Sally and Albert.
    D. She thought that people would laugh at her.

4. Why did Mrs. Johnson wave at April?
    A. She wanted April to thank the audience.
    B. She wanted April to smile for the camera.
    C. She wanted to say hello to April.
    D. She was trying to tell April to hold up her sign.

Gorillas

A **fact** is something that you know is true. An **opinion** is what you believe about something.

Gorillas live in the mountains and forests of Zaire, in Africa. Because they are peaceful animals, scientists can study them. Scientists found that gorillas live in groups made up of several females, their babies, and one or more males. A baby gorilla does not live with its mother long. After three years, it sets off on its own. That seems like a short time. Each evening, gorillas build nests to sleep in by picking leaves and laying down on them. Gorillas eat foods that include fruits, leaves, and juicy stems. They probably enjoy their food. Gorillas are becoming extinct because their forests are being destroyed. Many people are trying to save these forests and mountains. We should help save these forests and mountains, too!

Write three facts from the passage.

1. _____

2. _____

3. _____

Write three opinions from the passage.

4. _____

5. _____

6. _____

Summer Bridge Reading RB-904092

A Whale of a Tale

Color the facts green and the opinions blue.

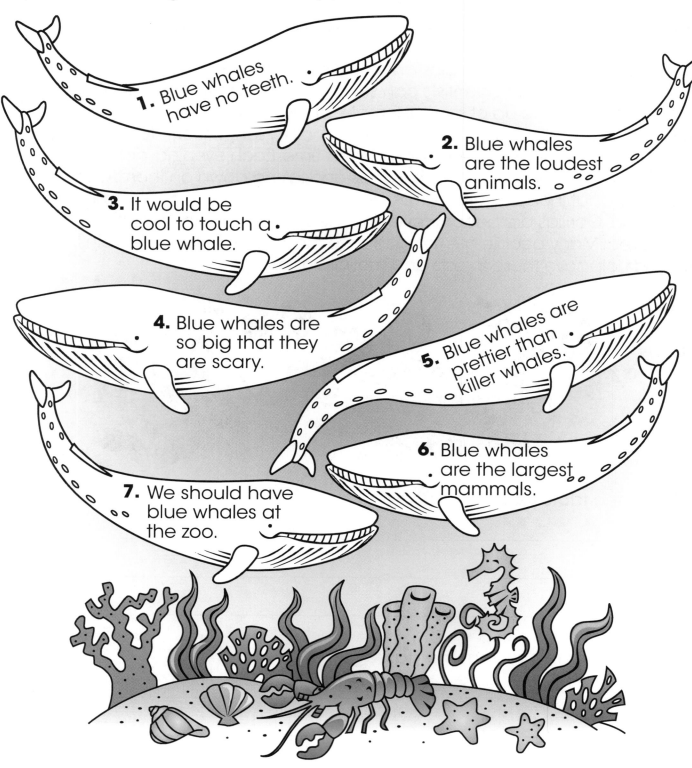

1. Blue whales have no teeth.

2. Blue whales are the loudest animals.

3. It would be cool to touch a blue whale.

4. Blue whales are so big that they are scary.

5. Blue whales are prettier than killer whales.

6. Blue whales are the largest mammals.

7. We should have blue whales at the zoo.

Snowboarding

Read the passage below.

What sport can make you feel like you are flying? Try snowboarding. It's a little like surfing. It's a little like skateboarding. It's a little like skiing, too. To snowboard, you stand on one board and quickly glide down a snowy hill.

A snowboard is shaped like a skateboard, but it is longer and wider. It does not have wheels. It is made of fiberglass, wood, plastic, and metal. Snowboards come in many shapes, sizes, and colors. A beginner usually uses a short, wide board.

Snowboarders wear special boots that snap onto snowboards. Most people ride with the left foot in front. The toes point inward a little. You can turn the board by leaning on your toes or heels. Turning on a snowboard is called edging.

Like any sport, snowboarding takes practice. Many ski slopes allow people to snowboard. But, before they do, snowboarders must learn safety tips and rules.

Expert snowboarders can do special tricks. These people are very skilled. They are not beginners. They can ride backward. They can spin, flip, jump, and do tricks. There are many tricks, but some experts just want to go fast down a mountain.

Summer Bridge Reading RB-904092

Circle *fact* or *opinion* after each statement.

1. Snowboarding is as fun as flying.   fact   opinion

2. Snowboarding is like skateboarding in snow.   fact   opinion

3. Experts can do special tricks.   fact   opinion

4. Going fast is the most fun.   fact   opinion

5. Most people ride with the left foot in front.   fact   opinion

6. You shouldn't do tricks until you are 16 years old.   fact   opinion

7. Only boys can go snowboarding.   fact   opinion

Extra!

Put these words in the puzzle. Some of the letters have already been filled in for you.

spin

ollie

grab

wheelie

backward

Forest Animals

Classifying means putting things into groups. One way to make groups is by days, months, or years. Your photo album may be classified by time.

Read "Forest Animals."

Many kinds of animals live in the forest. Some forest animals are very small. They have six legs. They are insects. Butterflies, ants, beetles, and bees are insects.

Some forest animals spend their entire lives in lakes or streams. They have scales. They breathe through gills. They are fish. Trout, bass, and catfish are fish.

Other forest animals are reptiles and amphibians. Amphibians spend part of their lives in the water and part of their lives on the land. Frogs and toads are amphibians. Snakes, lizards, and turtles are reptiles.

Look at the names of the animals in each list. Look at the titles in the box. Write the correct title on each line.

amphibians	reptiles	insects	fish

1. _____

   trout

   bass

2. _____

   frogs

   toads

3. _____

   butterflies

   bees

4. _____

   snakes

   lizards

Does It Belong?

To help you find the thing that does not belong in a group, look for what the others have in common.
Example: ball, doll, puzzle, pencil (The pencil does not fit because it is not a toy.)

Cross out the word that does not belong in each group.

1.	2.	3.	4.
apple	whale	boat	boots
banana	bobcat	car	hat
potato	squirrel	airplane	mittens
watermelon	raccoon	road	snowman

5.	6.	7.	8.
towel	cotton	candle	bitter
soap	rock	flashlight	sour
shampoo	pillow	mirror	lemon
shoes	feather	lantern	sweet

9.	10.	11.	12.
star	piano	maple	wagon
moon	drum	rose	sled
rocket	song	daisy	scooter
planet	guitar	sunflower	bike

Extra!
Go outside or look out a window. Make a list of 15 things you see outside. Then, divide the list into 3 groups. Give each group a name.

My Day

Classify your day into three groups: morning, afternoon, and evening. Write three activities that belong in each group.

My Morning

1. _____
2. _____
3. _____

My Afternoon

4. _____
5. _____
6. _____

My Evening

7. _____
8. _____
9. _____

Changing with the Seasons

Read the passage below.

Humans are not the only ones to change our clothes with the seasons. We change the way we dress with the seasons to protect us from the weather. Animals do the same thing to protect themselves from the weather. They know when the weather will change.

For example, the arctic fox has a thick, white fur coat in the winter. It is not easy to see in the snow. This helps the fox to hide from enemies. When spring comes, the fox's fur changes to brown. It is then the color of the ground.

The Ptarmigan bird, or White Chicken, has white feathers in the winter. It, too, is hard to see in the snow. In the spring, the bird molts. This means that it sheds all of its feathers. The bird grows new feathers that are speckled. When the bird is very still, it looks like a rock.

Changing with the Seasons

Answer the following questions using the passage on page 56.

1. What is "Changing with the Seasons" mostly about?

    A. how people change

    B. how seasons change

    C. how animals change in seasons

2. What color is the arctic fox's fur in the winter?

    A. brown

    B. white

    C. black

3. What happens to the Ptarmigan bird in the spring?

    A. It molts.

    B. It flies south.

    C. Its feathers turn red.

4. The word *molts* means:

    A. to change colors.

    B. to shed feathers.

    C. to hide from an enemy.

5. Draw a line to divide the two words that make up each compound word.

    A. springtime

    B. wintertime

    C. bluebird

6. What words could you type into a search engine or look up in a book to read more about how animals change each season?

_____

_____

_____

Summer Bridge Reading RB-904092

Alice Smith, Private Eye

> To make an **inference** means to make an educated guess using the information given.

Read the story below.

Alice hung a sign outside her clubhouse door. It read,

Alice Smith, Private Eye

Ned, her neighbor, rode down the driveway. He was on his tricycle. He looked at the sign for a long time. Then, he looked around the yard.

"Where is the yard sale?" he asked.

"There is no yard sale," said Alice. "That sign says that I am a detective. I solve crimes, and I find things that are lost."

"If I lost something, could you find it?" Ned asked.

"I could try," said Alice.

Ned took Alice to his house. They went to his room.

Alice looked around. She was not surprised that Ned had lost something. She was surprised that he ever found anything.

Ned went to his closet. He took out a plastic car. It had a slot in the top.

"This is my bank," he said. "Every week, I get 10 dimes for my allowance. I spend five of them at the arcade. I put the other five in here. On Monday, I had a lot of dimes. Now, they are all gone. Can you find them for me?"

"First, we need some clues," Alice said. She shook the bank. She did not hear any dimes. She opened the little door on the bottom of the bank. Two pieces of paper fell out. One was white. One was green. When she read what was written on the white paper, she tried not to laugh.

It said,

"Dear Ned,
I needed some change for the wash. You had $4.70 in dimes. Here is $5.00. Thank you.

Love, Mom"

Alice Smith, Private Eye

Answer the following questions using the story on page 58.

1. Why do most people post homemade signs on Alice's street?

_____

2. Was Ned's room messy or neat? How do you know?

_____

3. What was the green piece of paper in Ned's bank?

_____

4. Does Ned's mom own a washing machine that works?

_____

59

Missing Pen Mystery

Read the story below.

Mrs. Rochester asked her students if they had seen her favorite blue pen with stars on it. Hector looked at Kyla and whispered, "It sounds like a mystery."

During recess, Hector talked to Mrs. Rochester. "May we look at the crime scene?" There was a brown spot on the clean desk.

Kyla asked Mrs. Rochester if she had eaten any chocolate that day.

"No," sighed Mrs. Rochester, "but I wish I had some now."

Hector looked in the trash can. Kyla and Hector looked at all of the students' faces as they walked in the door.

After school, they went to see Mr. Bridges. Mr. Bridges loved chocolate. Kyla and Hector saw Mr. Bridges in the hallway. He had a blue pen in his pocket.

"Is that your pen, Mr. Bridges?" asked Hector.

"Well, no," he said as he patted his pocket. "I borrowed it from someone."

"Did you find it on Mrs. Rochester's desk?" asked Kyla.

"Yes, I did. I guess I forgot to give it back to her."

"Case closed," said the detectives.

Missing Pen Mystery

Answer the following questions using the story on page 60.

1. Why did Kyla and Hector ask about chocolate? _____

    _____

2. What was the brown spot on Mrs. Rochester's desk? _____

    _____

3. Why were Hector and Kyla looking at the students' faces? _____

    _____

4. How do you think Mr. Bridges got the pen? _____

    _____

Draw the pen.

Summer Bridge Reading RB-904092

Playing Outside

Read the story below.

Carla and Lucas played outside. The morning sun felt warm on Carla's head. She could smell the flowers that grew next to the house. She picked some ripe strawberries and shared them with Lucas. Carla laughed when Lucas smeared the berries on his cheek and chin.

Lucas played in the sandbox. He pushed the truck in the sand and made a noise with his mouth. Later, he pointed at the swing. Carla picked Lucas up and set him in the blue swing. She put on his seat belt and gave him a gentle push. Lucas laughed. Carla sat on the swing next to him and counted the red flowers by the house. "When I grow up, I want to take care of plants," said Carla.

"More!" said Lucas. Carla got up and pushed the swing.

"It's almost time for lunch," said Carla. "Mom is making us a picnic. Are you hungry?"

"More!" said Lucas.

62

Playing Outside

Answer the following questions using the story on page 62. Circle each answer.

1. How old do you think Lucas is?

one year old   four years old   eight years old

2. How old do you think Carla is?

one year old   eight years old   grown up

3. What is Lucas?

a boy   a dog   a girl

4. What are Lucas and Carla?

friends   siblings   classmates

5. What does Carla like to do?

paint   garden   cook

6. What does Lucas like to do?

talk   paint   swing

7. What time of day is it?

lunchtime   afternoon   night

8. What time of year is it?

fall   summer   winter

Summer Bridge Reading RB-904092

Kate and Her Dad

Read the story below.

Kate loves doing things with her dad. He is her best friend. Her dad loves to play basketball. He is on a team. Kate loves to play basketball. She is on a team, too. Her dad is the coach of her team. Sometimes after a game, Kate and her dad go out for ice cream. They both have chocolate fudge ice cream.

Sometimes before dinner, Kate and her dad go for a run. They run around the track at the neighborhood school. Kate enjoys running with her dad. Sometimes, they talk when they run. Sometimes, they just run.

At bedtime, Kate's dad always tucks her in. Kate's dad tells her stories. Her favorite stories are about when her dad was a little boy. Next, her dad talks with her about what happened during the day. Then, he kisses her gently on the forehead. Kate thinks her dad is the greatest.

Kate and Her Dad

Answer the following questions using the story on page 64.

1. What is this story mainly about?

   A. having fun

   B. why Kate loves her dad

   C. eating ice cream

2. Write three things Kate enjoys doing with her dad.

_____

_____

_____

3. Read the sentences below. Write *S* if the statement is stated in the story. Write *I* if the statement is inferred in the story. Inferred means something isn't told exactly, but you get the idea from what is stated.

___ Kate's dad plays on a basketball team.

___ Kate's dad loves her.

___ Kate's dad tucks her in.

___ Kate and her dad like to talk.

Write the plural of each word.

4. story _____

5. kiss _____

6. hug _____

7. friend _____

8. cone _____

9. neighbor _____

10. boy _____

11. girl _____

12. Draw a line to divide the two words that make up each compound word.

   A. basketball

   B. bedtime

   C. neighborhood

   D. sometimes

Summer Bridge Reading RB-904092

What Will Happen?

You can predict what will happen next by using the clues within a story.

Use the clues from each story to predict what happens next. Circle the sentence that tells what probably happened next.

My three-year-old brother, Zach, is crazy! He has a mind of his own, and he likes to do things he shouldn't! This morning, we took him to the park, and I told Mom that I would keep an eye on him. On our way there, Zach spotted a flower and wanted to pick it for me. I told him that we should leave the flower for everyone to enjoy. As soon as I turned around, _____.

Zach gave me a hug.

Zach asked me to swing with him.

Zach picked the flower.

I chased Zach to the playground. He wanted to slide down the big slide. I told him to wait until I said, "Go!" so that I could catch him at the bottom. I ducked under the slide to get ready. Suddenly, I heard Zach laughing. I looked up, and _____.

I saw Zach coming down the slide.

I saw a blue jay fly by.

I saw kids tickling Zach.

Soon, it was time for lunch. Mom brought sandwiches, chips, and lemonade. Zach found some cookies in the basket, too. I asked him not to eat all of them because I wanted one for the ride home. Later, as we jumped in the car, I reached for a cookie. I should have known that _____.

Zach had fallen asleep.

Zach had muddy shoes.

Zach had eaten all of the cookies.

What a Character!

Some stories give you clues about characters without ever telling you who they are.

Use the clues in the poem to guess the character.

Who's there? Was that the breeze? Or is something hiding behind those trees?

Who's there? I heard a sound. I see eyes that are big and round.

Who's there? Come along! I see four legs, big and strong.

Who's there? The light is dim, but I don't think that you will swim.

Who's there? Did you hear me call? You don't look very small.

Who's there? Can you fly? I see a tail going low and high.

Who's there? Should I hide from sight? I see whiskers that are long and white.

Who's there? Come back! I see something orange and black.

One of these characters fits all of the clues in the poem. Circle it.

Opal's Dance

Read the story below.

Opal is known throughout the sea as one of the most talented creatures. She has been tap dancing for as long as she can remember. Opal is an octopus. When you watch her tap dance, you are in for four times the show you would see if you were watching someone with only two legs. Her fans come from oceans far, far away to see her.

It was a special night for Opal. She was dancing for King Manatee and his family. King Manatee traveled many miles to watch Opal dance. Princess Paige, the king's daughter, wanted to be a dancer just like Opal. It was Paige's birthday wish to watch Opal tap dance.

Usually, Opal was comfortable in all of her shows. But, this show was a little different. She could not eat a bite of her dinner. When her friend, Logan Lobster, asked her what was wrong, she told him that she had never performed in front of royalty before. Opal was nervous. Logan calmed her down by talking to her and keeping her company until it was time for Opal to get dressed. But, that was when the real problem began.

"Logan!" Opal screamed from her dressing room. "There are only seven tap shoes in my closet! I can't find my other shoe!"

"Are you sure?" Logan asked. "They were all here last night when you performed for the Tuna family."

"I know," replied Opal. "I can't imagine what happened to that shoe. Oh, what should I do?"

Opal put on her other seven shoes and gave tapping a try in her dressing room. "It's no use," she cried. "We will have to cancel the show. I can't dance with only seven shoes. It will ruin the rhythm of the routines." Logan went out to break the bad news.

Just after he left, Opal heard a tiny voice. "Maybe I can help," the voice said.

"Who said that?" Opal asked.

"It's me, Callie." Opal looked down to see her neighbor, Callie Clam, peeking into her dressing room door. "I'm tiny, but I have very big ideas," Callie said. Opal listened to Callie's plan.

Just in time, Callie and Opal caught up with Logan. "Don't cancel the show," Opal said. "Callie has a plan, and I think it just might work!"

They shared the idea with Logan. "Let's give it a try," he said.

Opal danced better than she had ever danced before. She was given three standing ovations, and on the third, she spoke. "Your majesties, I must tell you what an honor it has been to dance for you. I must also tell you that I did not perform alone tonight." At that moment, Opal took something off of the bottom of one of her tentacles. It was Callie! She continued, "I would like to introduce you to my dear friend, Callie Clam. You see, I couldn't find one of my tap shoes tonight, and Callie had a great idea. She suggested that I tape her to the bottom of one of my regular shoes. Then, she would make a tapping sound just like the other shoes. We tried it, and it worked."

Callie smiled at the princess and said, "It's a pleasure to meet you."

"Likewise," said Princess Paige.

The king was pleased that his daughter's heroine and Callie had been able to demonstrate such teamwork. He decided to do something special for Opal and Callie. The king had a brand new dance studio built for Opal. In the front row, he built a special chair, taller than the rest, for Callie. Every year, the king and his family returned for Paige's birthday, just to watch Opal dance.

Opal's Dance

After reading "Opal's Dance," answer the following questions.

1. Number the sentences to put the events in the correct order.
   ___ Opal was given three standing ovations for her show.
   ___ Opal couldn't find one of her shoes.
   ___ Callie, Opal, and Paige became friends.
   ___ Callie had a plan to help Opal.
   ___ The king was pleased with Opal and Callie's teamwork.

2. Why was the night in the story a special night for Opal?
   A. It was her birthday.
   B. She and Logan became friends.
   C. She was dancing for King Manatee and his family.
   D. She was singing a new song for the king.

3. How did Callie help Opal?
   A. She brought her dinner on the night of her big show.
   B. She let Opal tape her to her shoe so that the shoe would make a tapping sound.
   C. She helped Opal learn her new dance routine.
   D. She introduced Opal to King Manatee and Princess Paige.

4. What did the king do for Callie?
   A. He came to watch Opal dance every year.
   B. He built a new dance studio.
   C. He took everyone out to dinner.
   D. He built her a special tall chair in the front row of the new dance studio.

5. What do you think happened to Opal's shoe?

_____

_____

Summer Bridge Reading RB-904092

Mount Kilimanjaro

It is important to read directions one at a time and follow them exactly. Sometimes, it is helpful to check them off as you work.

Follow each step in the directions below. Mark each step with an *X* as you complete it.

Mount Kilimanjaro is in Africa. Follow the directions below to complete the map of the area around Mount Kilimanjaro.

___ Draw a farmer and a bird in the grasslands.

___ Color the grasslands yellow.

___ Draw a monkey, leopard, and lion in the tropical forest.

___ Color the tropical forest dark green.

___ Draw an elephant, buffalo, and eagle in the low alpine.

___ Color the low alpine light green.

___ Draw a spider and an insect in the high alpine.

___ Color the high alpine brown.

___ Color the summit white.

72

The Great Race

Find a friend and play this game.

What You Will Need:
Coin
Space Markers

Object of the Game:
To be the first to cross the finish line

How to Play:
The youngest player goes first.

Flip a coin. Move one space for heads. Move two spaces for tails. Follow the directions on each space.

Start	Slow start. Go back 1 space.	Great start! Go ahead 2 spaces.			Tripped on shoelace. Go back 1 space.	
			Running strong. Take another turn.			
	Record time. Go ahead 3 spaces.		Leg cramps. Lose a turn.			
				Getting tired. Go back 3 spaces.		
	Missed a hurdle. Go back 2 spaces.					**Finish**

Summer Bridge Reading RB-904092

The Great Race

Answer the following questions using the activity on page 73.

1. What is the main idea?
   - **A.** how to play a game
   - **B.** how to run in a race
   - **C.** how to be in first place

2. Who goes first?
   - **A.** the owner of the game
   - **B.** the biggest person
   - **C.** the youngest person

3. What is the object of the game?
   - **A.** to not trip when running a race
   - **B.** to be the first to cross the finish line
   - **C.** to get the best start

4. What is the consequence of each action?
   - **A.** tripped on shoelace

   _____

   - **B.** getting tired

   _____

   - **C.** missed a hurdle

   _____

Read this game box. Answer the questions below.

A Rainbow Bridge Game

Hop to It!
The game that keeps you on your toes

For 3 or more players
For ages 5 to adult

5. What is the game's name?

   _____

6. How old do you need to be to play the game? _____

7. Can two people play the game? _____

Write the base word for the following words:

8. tripped _____

9. running _____

10. getting _____

11. tired _____

12. crossed _____

Treasure Map

Ben and Matt were playing pirates. While digging for treasure, they found this map. Follow the directions to find the treasure. Mark an *X* where the treasure is buried.

Start in the Red River Valley.

Go northeast to the Black Forest.

Go northeast to the next forest.

Travel north to the Purple Mountains.

Cross the Red River to the Blue Mountains.

Go south, but do not cross the Red River again.

The treasure is buried here.

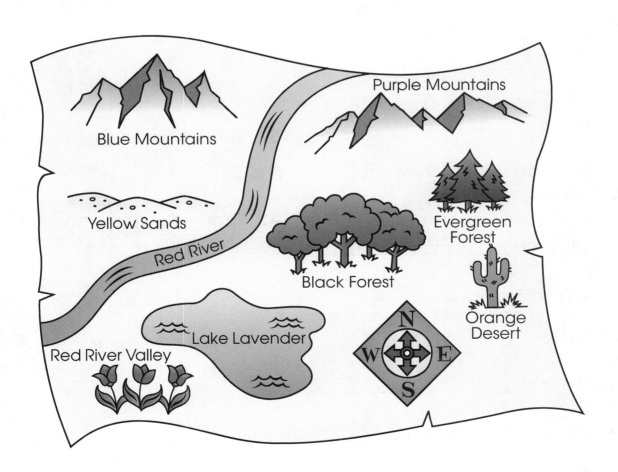

Summer Bridge Reading RB-904092

Treasure Map

Answer the following questions using the treasure map on page 75.

1. Where is the treasure buried?

   _____

2. When you go northeast from the Black Forest, what forest do you find?

   _____

3. Draw a line from the color to the place as noted on the map.

Yellow	Mountains
Orange	River
Red	Sands
Purple	Desert

Write the base word for each word below.

4. playing _____

5. digging _____

6. buried _____

7. missing _____

8. hunting _____

Cross out the word that does not belong in each group.

9. | blue | yellow |
   |---|---|
   | red | sky |

10. | forest | mountains |
    |---|---|
    | tree | desert |

11. | north | left |
    |---|---|
    | south | east |

12. | desert | ocean |
    |---|---|
    | river | lake |

13. | mountain | hill |
    |---|---|
    | leak | valley |

14. Draw your own map. Write directions for a friend to follow.

Is It Real?

Some stories are about things that can really happen. These are **reality** stories. Some stories are about things that could not really happen. These are **fantasy** stories.

Color the blocks that could be fact yellow. Color the blocks that are fantasy green.

1. Once upon a time, there was a princess named Anna.	**2.** One day, Anna lost her favorite ball in the lake.	**3.** She started to cry. Suddenly, a frog jumped out of the lake.	**4.** "Hello," he said. "I'll get your ball if you promise to take me home."
5. Anna agreed. The frog jumped in and threw the ball to her.	**6.** "Now I can return to the castle with you," the frog said.	**7.** Princess Anna laughed and ran back to the palace without the frog.	**8.** The frog was angry that Anna had broken her promise.
9. The frog went to the palace and knocked on the door.	**10.** The frog told the king how Anna had broken her promise.	**11.** The king said to Anna, "You must always keep your promises."	**12.** So the frog ate dinner from Anna's plate. "Yummy," he said.
13. Then, the frog put on his pajamas and jumped into bed.	**14.** Anna began to cry. Suddenly, the frog turned into a prince.	**15.** Anna and the prince became friends.	**16.** Anna learned to always keep her promises.

Fantastic Facts

By changing something that could really happen into something that could not really happen, you can change reality into fantasy.

Write the next sentence for each story idea, and turn it into fantasy.

1. The clock struck midnight.

_____

_____

2. My dog had been playing in the mud!

_____

_____

3. I looked in my desk at school.

_____

_____

4. The girl looked more closely at the butterfly.

_____

_____

Three Wishes

Read the story below.

A long time ago, there lived an old woman and an old man. They didn't have much money. But, they did have a fine cottage and enough food to eat. One day, they went fishing. They sat on the shore for hours without one bite. Suddenly, the man felt a tug on his line. He reeled in a fish. What a big fish it was! Surely, the fish would have fed him and his wife for a whole week. But as he began to unhook the fish, the fish spoke!

"Please let me go," said the fish. "If you do, I will grant you three wishes."

"A talking fish!" shouted the old man. "How can this be?" And without thinking, he threw the fish back into the water.

The little old woman shouted, "You foolish man! You threw the fish back without making any wishes. And, you threw back a fish that could feed us for a week. Just once I wish you would think!"

As the words came out of the woman's mouth, a thought popped into the man's mind. "Well," said the man, "your wish has come true. I am thinking. I am thinking that you are a rude woman, and I wish you would keep quiet!"

And just as the man wished, the woman's mouth was shut tight. The old couple sat and stared at each other. "What have we done?" the man said. "With three wishes, we could have wished for money, food, or fame, but instead we wished away our wishes. Now, the only sensible wish would be that my wife's mouth would be opened."

As quickly as the man said the last wish, the woman's mouth was opened. "We don't have more money or food or fame, but we do have each other. That is enough," said the old man. Together, the old woman and the old man walked back to their house.

Three Wishes

Answer the following questions using the story on page 79.

1. What is the main idea?
   A. Be careful not to catch talking fish.
   B. Think before you speak.
   C. Always be ready with three wishes.

2. How would you describe this story?
   A. serious
   B. true
   C. silly

Read the sentences. Write *T* if a sentence might be true. Write *F* if it is fantasy.

3. _____ A long time ago, there lived an old man and an old woman.

4. _____ The couple went fishing.

5. _____ The man caught a talking fish.

6. _____ Because of a wish, the woman's mouth shut tight.

7. _____ The couple walked back to their house.

A **homophone** is a word that sounds the same as another word, but has a different spelling and meaning. Write a homophone from the story for each word below.

8. ours _____

9. real _____

10. weak _____

11. bee _____

12. through _____

Use correct punctuation at the end of each sentence.

13. Have you ever seen a talking fish ___

14. Why, it's a talking fish ___

15. My dad caught a fish ___

16. Can you go fishing with me ___

17. I like to go fishing with my dad ___

Samantha's Gift

Reading carefully will help you watch for parts of a story that are **alike** (similarities) and parts that are **different** (differences). Read the story below and watch for similarities and differences.

Mrs. Sanders and Mr. Sanders were very happy with their daughter's most recent report card. They wanted to get her a special gift for all of her hard work.

Mrs. Sanders thought they should take Samantha to eat at her favorite restaurant, but Mr. Sanders disagreed. He thought they should take her to see a movie.

Mr. and Mrs. Sanders went to visit Samantha's teacher. Her teacher told them that Samantha's soccer coach might know what she would want.

Then, Mr. and Mrs. Sanders went to visit Samantha's soccer coach. He recommended that they ask Samantha's best friend what would be a good reward.

Finally, Mr. and Mrs. Sanders went to visit Samantha's best friend, Kelly. She said, "I think Samantha would like to do both."

Mr. and Mrs. Sanders thought it was a brilliant idea. They invited Kelly to go, too. They all went to dinner and a movie together and had a great time.

Label each sentence with *S* if it shows a similarity and *D* if it shows a difference.

_____ **1.** Samantha's teacher and soccer coach sent Mr. and Mrs. Sanders to see someone else.

_____ **2.** Mr. Sanders wanted to take Samantha to see a movie. Mrs. Sanders wanted to take her to eat at her favorite restaurant.

_____ **3.** Mr. and Mrs. Sanders wanted to give Samantha a gift for her hard work in school.

Summer Bridge Reading RB-904092

Rebecca and Neela

Read the story below. Then, answer the questions.

Rebecca and Neela are best friends. They have the same haircut. They wear the same clothes. They love to read. Both girls have their own pet. Rebecca has a bird. Neela has a mouse. Rebecca lets her bird, Jade, fly around her room. Neela keeps her mouse, Julius, in his cage. Rebecca and Neela take good care of their pets.

1. What do Rebecca and Neela love to do? _____

2. How do the girls look alike? _____

   _____

3. What is different about the girls? _____

   _____

4. How do they play differently with their pets? _____

   _____

82

Alligators & Crocodiles

Read the passage below.

Is that a log in the water? It doesn't seem to be moving. But, are those eyes? Watch out! It's an alligator! Or is it a crocodile? Many people confuse alligators and crocodiles. They look and act very much the same.

Alligators and crocodiles live in the water. They eat fish, turtles, birds, and other animals. Crocodiles have pointed snouts. Alligators have wide, rounded snouts. The upper jaw of the alligator is wider than its lower jaw. When its mouth is closed, most of its teeth are hidden. The upper and lower jaws of the crocodile are about the same size. Many of its teeth can be seen when its mouth is closed.

Crocodiles and alligators are cold-blooded. Cold-blooded animals stay cool in the water and warm in the sun. Alligators prefer to live in fresh water. Crocodiles are often found in salt water.

People may think that alligators and crocodiles are slow because they lie so still in the water. But, they can move fast on land with their short legs. Both animals are fierce. Stay away! They can be dangerous.

Summer Bridge Reading RB-904092

Alligators & Crocodiles

Complete the Venn diagram to describe alligators and crocodiles. Use the phrases in the Fact Bank.

Fact Bank

eat fish

live in the water

have pointed snouts

have rounded snouts

show many teeth when jaws are closed

prefer fresh water

warm up in the sun

cool off in the water

can move fast

are fierce

have wider upper jaws than lower jaws

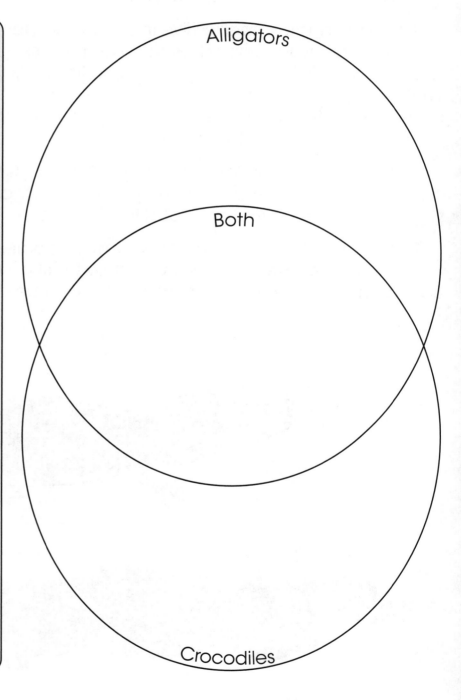

84

Stay Safe

Read the passage below.

Trains go almost everywhere. There are almost 200,000 miles (315,000 km) of train tracks in the United States. There might be train tracks near your house. If there are, you need to learn a few rules so that you can stay safe.

Trains are big and heavy. It is dangerous to walk on train tracks. Even if an engineer sees you, it can take more than a mile to stop the train.

Sometimes, people walk on or next to railroad tracks when they take shortcuts. They think they will know when a train is coming. They are wrong. They may not know when a train is coming since trains run at all times.

When you must cross train tracks, go to a special crossing. Watch all of the signs. Never go around a gate that is down. Never cross the tracks when lights are flashing. Trains can be very fast and quiet. You may not hear one coming until it is too late.

Remember: Cross at special crossings. Pay attention to the signs. Don't walk on or play near train tracks. Stay safe!

Stay Safe

Answer the following questions using the passage on page 85. Read the sentences. Circle *T* if a sentence is true. Circle *F* if it is false.

1. One purpose of "Stay Safe" is to teach people how to ride bikes.　　　　T　　　F

2. One purpose of "Stay Safe" is to tell the history of trains.　　　　T　　　F

3. One purpose of "Stay Safe" is to teach safety around railroad tracks.　　　　T　　　F

4. One purpose of "Stay Safe" is to keep people from getting hurt.　　　　T　　　F

5. One purpose of "Stay Safe" is to sell train tickets.　　　　T　　　F

6. One purpose of "Stay Safe" is to tell when trains run.　　　　T　　　F

7. One purpose of "Stay Safe" is to make people laugh.　　　　T　　　F

Read the passage below.

Have you ever played charades? Charades is a fun game to play with a group of friends. All you need to play is a pencil and paper.

Split players into two teams. Each team writes down book, movie, and song titles on little pieces of paper. Each team's pieces of paper are then put into a different bowl. One person takes a piece of paper from the other team's bowl. That person must act out the title. Her team must guess what the title is.

First, the player shows the team whether it is a movie, song, or book. The player cannot talk or make sounds. Only hand and body motions are allowed. With his fingers, the player shows how many words are in the title. Then, the team watches the player act out the words. The team members must guess and shout out their answers.

Everyone gets a turn. Both teams play. The winning team guesses the most correct titles.

Charades

Answer the following questions using the passage on page 87. Circle your answers.

1. Why was this passage written?
   A. to make you laugh
   B. to teach you something
   C. to convince you to buy something

2. What is the reason for the picture?
   A. to help you understand
   B. to make you laugh
   C. so you don't have to read

3. What do you need to play charades?
   A. a game board
   B. money
   C. paper and a pencil

4. How many people can play the game?
   A. two
   B. three
   C. a crowd

5. What do players write on their papers?
   A. their names
   B. funny stories
   C. titles

6. What can't you use when you play charades?
   A. body motions
   B. your voice
   C. your hands

Basketball

> **Summarizing** means to tell the main point of a story.

Read the passage below.

Basketball is fun. To play, you need a ball and two baskets. There are two teams. Each team tries to put the ball in their basket. This is called shooting. One team starts with the ball. The players on that team try to score points. They pass the ball to each other. The other team tries to stop them from scoring. They try to take away the ball.

A basket is worth two points. If a player who is shooting the ball gets pushed, a foul is called. The player who was pushed gets two free throws. A free throw is worth one point. The game lasts four quarters. Each quarter is 12 minutes long. The team with the most points at the end wins the game. Everybody cheers for the winners. The teams shake hands.

Write a word from the passage to complete each summary sentence.

1. Basketball is a game played with _____ teams.

2. To play, you need a ball and two _____.

3. The _____ on each team try to score points.

4. A basket is _____ points. A free throw is _____ point.

5. The team with the _____ points at the end of the game wins.

Summer Bridge Reading RB-904092

Nursery Rhymes

Read the summaries. Write the name of the nursery rhyme that each summary describes.

1. Once, there was a cat who played the violin. She played in the farmyard all night long. The other animals danced and sang along with her. One night, the cow danced so happily, she jumped over the moon. The animals were very excited. The dog laughed loudly. The ground shook with all of the dancing. Even the dishes and spoons seemed to run on the kitchen shelves.

Nursery Rhyme

_____

2. On a summer day, the county fair was busy with people. The children rode ponies. Cakes and pies were for sale at the market. A boy named Simon asked for a taste of pie. The man selling the pies asked him for a penny. Simon did not have any money. The man sent him away.

Nursery Rhyme

_____

Super T Man

> **Idioms** are sayings that have different meanings than the words used to make them.
> **Example:** *Look before you leap* means to think before you act.

Read "Super T Man." Then, circle the correct answers to the questions.

José saw his friend, Miguel, standing in front of the toy store window at the mall. Miguel looked sad.

"What's wrong?" José asked.

Miguel pointed to an action figure. "They have Super T Man," he said.

"That's great!" said José. He had been waiting for the Super T Man figure for two months. He knew Miguel had been waiting for it, too.

"I don't have enough money," said Miguel. "I spent all of it at the school fair last week."

"Well, don't cry over spilled milk," said José. "I'll buy it today. We'll share it until you get your own."

"Super J Man is better anyway," said Miguel. "Super J Man is my friend José!"

1. What did Miguel want?
    A. He wanted some milk.
    B. He wanted a Super T Man action figure.
    C. He wanted a baseball.

2. Why couldn't Miguel buy the action figure?
    A. They were all gone.
    B. His father would not let him.
    C. He didn't have enough money.

3. What does the saying, "Don't cry over spilled milk" mean?
    A. When something is over, stop thinking about it.
    B. Do not spill milk.
    C. Do not cry.

4. How did José help?
    A. He gave Miguel money.
    B. He bought the action figure and shared it.
    C. He gave Miguel the action figure.

The Same Meaning

Read each paragraph. Then, circle the meaning of the bold saying.

1. Jonathan worked all day on a kite for Kite Day at the park. He did not use a kit. He made his kite from sticks, tissue paper, and string. He took it to an open field behind his house. He lifted it up. The wind caught it. It went straight up. It came straight down. Two sticks were broken. "Well, I guess **it's back to the drawing board**," Jonathan said.

   A. He had to make his new kite on a drawing board.

   B. He had to start over again.

   C. His kite broke because he did not draw plans.

2. Teresa and Becca wanted to be in the school talent show. They chose a good song. They practiced it every day for two weeks. They even bought matching outfits. The night before the show, Teresa called Becca. Her voice was shaking.

   "**I'm getting cold feet**," she said. "I don't think I can sing tomorrow."

   "I know how you feel," said Becca. "I've done this before. I'm always scared the night before. Once I start singing, I'm fine. You will be, too."

   A. She was catching a cold.

   B. She needed warmer socks.

   C. She was starting to feel afraid.

Extra!

Unscramble the words in this saying.

Hint: It means to be right about something.

iHt   hte   anli   no   teh   deah

_ i _   _ _ _   n _ _ _   _ _   _ _ _   _ e _ _ .

Summer Bridge Reading RB-904092

Another Way to Say It

Read each paragraph. Then, circle the meaning of the bold saying.

1. Pete was a good pitcher, but he was a bad sport. When the umpire called for a walk, his face turned red. He threw his glove on the ground. He turned around and told the other players on his team that the game wasn't fair. Soon, all of the players on Pete's team started shouting that the game wasn't fair. The umpire blew his whistle. He said, "**One rotten apple spoils the barrel**. This game is over."

   A. Pete was throwing apples.

   B. The baseballs were in a barrel.

   C. One bad thing makes other things bad.

2. Shona and Jessica were best friends until Brianna moved in. Shona lived next door to Brianna's new house. She met Brianna first. Brianna was an actress. She had been on TV. She was also friendly and funny. Shona was proud to show her around. The next day, Shona walked to school with Brianna. Jessica saw them walk by her house. She ran to catch up. **Shona gave her the cold shoulder**.

   A. Shona's shoulders were cold.

   B. Shona pretended Jessica was not her friend.

   C. Shona sent Jessica home to get her a sweater.

Extra!

Circle the saying that means something is too old and worn out to be repaired.

It has a clean bill of health.

That is the last straw.

It is on its last legs.

Answer Key

Page 9

1. beautiful; 2. hat; 3. sleep;
4. hop; 5. laughs; 6. dark,
light; 7. day, night; 8. small,
big; 9. tall, short; 10. start, finish

Page 11

1. A.; 2. Wash your hands
with soap., Cover your
mouth when you cough
or sneeze., Get plenty of
sleep., Eat healthy meals.;
3. T, F, T; 4. i; 5. u; 6. u; 7. o;
8. noun; 9. Answers will vary.

Page 13

1. B.; 2. 4, 1, 3, 2; 3. B.; 4. o;
5. a; 6. a; 7. u; 8. noun;
9. verb; 10. noun; 11. verb;
12. noun; 13. verb

Page 14

1. hay; 2. paint; 3. weed;
4. beet; 5. light; 6. bean;
7. paid; 8. right; 9. coat;
10. coast; 11. beads; 12. meat;
13. goat; 14. read; 15. tray

Page 16

1. A.; 2. D.; 3. B.; 4. B.; 5. D.

Page 18

1. B; 2. T; 3. B; 4. G; 5. G;
6. Pictures will vary.;
7. fraternal; 8. base, teeth,
play, braces, both

Page 20

1. The Panda Keeper;
2. Becoming a Zookeeper;
3. When Yang Yang Is Sick;
4. What Yang Yang Eats

Page 21

1. C.; 2. B.; 3. A.

Page 22

1. C.; 2. B.; 3. A.

Page 23

1. C.; 2. B.; 3. A.

Page 24

Bookbag 6

Page 25

1. banana; 2. jelly or jam;
3. wings; 4. sausage links;
5. eyes

Page 26

1. True; 2. False; 3. True;
4. True; 5. True; 6. False;
7. False; Extra: Answers
will vary.

Page 27

triangles: Alex; rectangles:
Jessica; squares: Jessica;
cylinders: Jessica; cubes:
Alex; cones: Alex

Page 28

1. light; 2. piece; 3. couch;
4. piece; 5. small hills;
6. special; 7. quiet

Page 29

1. nice; 2. under; 3. pain;
4. big; 5. ruin; 6. get;
Extra: Answers will vary.

Page 30

1. carrots; 2. relief; 3. toughest;
4. thief; 5. emergency;
Extra: Answers will vary.

Page 31

1. clown; 2. smile; 3. balloons;
4. laugh; 5. night; 6. stars;
7. animals; 8. first

Page 33

1. C.; 2. B.; 3. A.; 4. C.; 5. B.;
6. California, United States,
Australia; 7. 5, 1, 6, 3, 4, 2, 7

Page 34

1. lazy; 2. mean; 3. selfish;
4. kind; 5. helpful; 6. strong

Page 35

1. City Mouse; 2. Country
Mouse; 3. Country Mouse;
4. City Mouse; 5. Country
Mouse; 6. City Mouse

Page 36

1. scared; 2. worried; 3. proud;
4. disappointed

Page 39

1. B.; 2. D.; 3. A.;
4. Answers will vary.;
5. Answers will vary.

Page 40

4, 1, 3, 6, 2, 5

Page 42

1. 8, 2, 1, 3, 7, 4, 5, 6;
2. sighed, laughed,
screamed, shouted,
squealed, bellowed,
snickered; 3. 6; 4. 350°F;
5. 10–12 minutes; 6. 2 dozen

Page 43

1. B.; 2. E.; 3. D.; 4. A.;
5. C.; 6. Answers will vary.

Page 44

1. C, E; 2. E, C; 3. C, E;
4. E, C; 5. C, E; Extra:
Answers will vary.

 Summer Bridge Reading RB-904092

Answer Key

Page 45

1. I came early.; 2. The glass fell on the floor.; 3. I felt sick.; 4. The grass was very wet.; 5. I fell in the river.; 6. The rabbit saw us.; 7. The weeds grew fast.; Extra: Answers will vary.

Page 48

1. C.; 2. B.; 3. D.; 4. A.

Page 49

1. Gorillas live in the mountains and the forests of Zaire; 2. Gorillas live in groups.; 3. Each evening, gorillas build nests to sleep in.; 4. They probably enjoy their food.; 5. A baby gorilla does not live with its mother long.; 6. We should help save these forests and mountains.

Page 50

1. fact; 2. fact; 3. opinion; 4. opinion; 5. opinion; 6. fact; 7. opinion

Page 52

1. opinion; 2. fact; 3. fact; 4. opinion; 5. fact; 6. opinion; 7. opinion

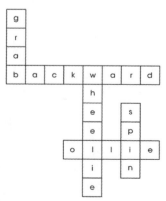

Page 53

1. fish; 2. amphibians; 3. insects; 4. reptiles

Page 54

1. potato; 2. whale; 3. road; 4. snowman; 5. shoes; 6. rock; 7. mirror; 8. lemon; 9. rocket; 10. song; 11. maple; 12. sled; Extra: Answers will vary.

Page 55

Answers will vary.

Page 57

1. C.; 2. B.; 3. A.; 4. B; 5. A. spring/time; B. winter/time; C. blue/bird; 6. Answers will vary.

Page 59

1. yard sales; 2. messy–Alice was surprised he ever found anything.; 3. $5.00 bill; 4. no

Page 61

1. The desk was clean except for a brown spot.; 2. chocolate; 3. to see if they had chocolate on their faces; 4. He borrowed the pen.; Drawings will vary.

Page 63

1. one year old; 2. eight years old; 3. a boy; 4. siblings; 5. garden; 6. swing; 7. lunchtime; 8. summer

Page 65

1. B.; 2. playing basketball, running, talking, eating ice cream; 3. S, I, S, I; 4. stories; 5. kisses; 6. hugs; 7. friends; 8. cones; 9. neighbors; 10. boys; 11. girls; 12. A. basket/ball; B. bed/time; C. neighbor/hood; D. some/times

Page 66

Zach picked the flower.; I saw Zach coming down the slide.; Zach had eaten all of the cookies.

Page 67

A tiger

Page 71

1. 3, 1, 5, 2, 4; 2. C.; 3. B.; 4. D.; 5. Answers will vary.

Page 72

Drawings should follow directions.

Page 74

1. A.; 2. C.; 3. B.; 4. A. Go back 1 space.; B. Go back 3 spaces.; C. Go back 2 spaces.; 5. Hop to It!; 6. 5 or older; 7. No; 8. trip; 9. run; 10. get; 11. tire; 12. cross

Page 75

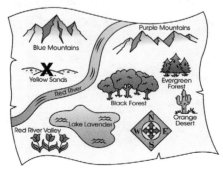

Answer Key

Page 76

1. Yellow Sands; 2. Evergreen Forest; 3. yellow, sands; orange, desert; red, river; purple, mountains; 4. play; 5. dig; 6. bury; 7. miss; 8. hunt; 9. sky; 10. tree; 11. left; 12. desert; 13. leak; 14. Answers will vary.

Page 77

1. yellow; 2. yellow; 3. yellow; 4. green; 5. green; 6. green; 7. yellow; 8. green; 9. green; 10. green; 11. yellow; 12. green; 13. green; 14. green; 15. yellow; 16. yellow

Page 78

Answers will vary.

Page 80

1. B.; 2. C.; 3. T; 4. T; 5. F; 6. F; 7. T; 8. hours; 9. reel; 10. week; 11. be; 12. threw; 13. (?); 14. (!); 15. (.); 16. (?); 17. (.)

Page 81

1. S; 2. D; 3. S

Page 82

1. read books; 2. same haircut and wear the same clothes; 3. their pets; 4. Rebecca lets her bird out of its cage. Neela keeps her mouse in its cage.

Page 84

Alligators: have rounded snouts, prefer fresh water, have wider upper jaws than lower jaws; Both: warm up in the sun, cool off in the water, eat fish, live in the water, can move fast, are fierce; Crocodiles: show many teeth when jaws are closed, have pointed snouts

Page 86

1. F; 2. F; 3. T; 4. T; 5. F; 6. F; 7. F

Page 88

1. B.; 2. A.; 3. C.; 4. C.; 5. C.; 6. B.

Page 89

1. two; 2. baskets/teams; 3. players; 4. two, one; 5. most

Page 90

1. Hey Diddle Diddle; 2. Simple Simon

Page 91

1. B.; 2. C.; 3. A.; 4. B.

Page 92

1. B.; 2. C.; Extra: Hit the nail on the head.

Page 93

1. C.; 2. B.; Extra: It is on its last legs.